The American Revolutionary Series

THE LOYALIST LIBRARY

*The American Revolutionary Series
is published in cooperation with
The Boston Public Library*

Tories
of
New Hampshire
in the
War of the Revolution

By
OTIS GRANT HAMMOND

With a New Introduction and Preface by
GEORGE ATHAN BILLIAS

GREGG PRESS
Boston 1972

This is a complete photographic reprint of a work
first published in Concord, New Hampshire,
by the New Hampshire Historical Society in 1917.
Reproduced from an original copy in the Boston Public Library.

First Gregg Press edition published 1972.

Printed on permanent/durable acid-free paper in
The United States of America.

Library of Congress Cataloging in Publication Data

Hammond, Otis Grant, 1869-1944.
    Tories of New Hampshire in the war of the revolution.

    (American Revolutionary series)
    Reprint of the 1917 ed.
    1. American loyalists—New Hampshire. I. Title.
II. Series.
E277.H22   1972   973.3'14   72-8758
ISBN 0-8398-0799-6

THE LOYALIST LIBRARY

THE LOYALISTS in the American Revolution represent one of the most misunderstood groups in our nation's history. For the past two centuries, they have fared badly at the hands of historians; Tories have either been neglected, or protrayed in an unsympathetic light by ultra-patriotic writers. The remark that a Loyalist was "a thing whose head is in England . . . body . . . in America, and its neck ought to be stretched," typifies the common attitude during the first century after the Revolution. This early period was one of outspoken nationalism, and resentment against the Loyalists and former mother country remained high. Although Anglo-American animosities diminished in the second century, and scholars adopted a more detached approach, the Tories were studied only sporadically. The present collection—called the Loyalist Library—contains both writings of important Tories and scholarly monographs on the subject. It should help to stimulate renewed research and interest in this forgotten part of America's past.

History is usually written by winners, not losers, and therefore we do not know as much about the Loyalists as we should. For one thing, we do not know how many Tories there actually were. The old estimate—mistakenly attributed to John Adams—claimed that the country was split three ways during the war: one-third becoming

Loyalists; one-third supporting the patriot cause; and one-third remaining neutral or indifferent. Modern scholars estimate that the Tories comprised something closer to nineteen percent of the total number of white Americans. Several studies included in this collection, such as Otis G. Hammond's *Tories of New Hampshire,* and Janet B. Johnson's biography of Robert Alexander, a Maryland Loyalist, provide evidence that casts serious doubts on the older assumption.

The Loyalist Library should help to correct another misconception—the idea that Tories came mainly from the upper class—from the ranks of royal officeholders, rich merchants, professional men, and well-to-do Anglicans. Recent research into the socio-economic background of Tories reveals that they hailed instead from the middle or lower classes in most of the colonies. Farmers, artisans, and small businessmen formed the backbone of the Loyalist movement for the most part. Wilbur H. Siebert's work on *The Loyalists of Pennsylvania,* for example, shows that in the Quaker colony many frontier farmers became Tories.

In geographical terms, the Loyalists were scattered throughout all of the original thirteen colonies. Virginia and Massachusetts had the smallest number. The strongest Tory support seems to have been in certain of the Middle Colonies—New York, New Jersey, and Pennsylvania—and in the South—in the Carolinas and Georgia. State studies of these areas, such as Edward Alfred Jones' *The Loyalists of New Jersey* and Harold B. Hancock's *The Delaware Loyalists,* tell us specifically who the Tories were—their names, place of residence, occupation or profession, and religion. Loyalists, moreover, tended to concentrate in urban areas and along the seacoast—except in New York, North Carolina, and parts of Pennsylvania where major pockets of Tories could be found in the interior. The treatment that Tories received at the hands of the Whigs in such seacoast cities as Boston may be gleaned from Arthur W. Eaton's biography of Mather Byles.

The Loyalist Library also provides proof that the Floridas and Nova Scotia—none of which rebelled—may have held the highest ratio of Tories. Wilbur H. Siebert's *Loyalists in East Florida, 1774 to 1785* indicates that the number of Tories in that colony increased substantially as a result of the exodus from the Carolinas and Georgia. The papers of Edward Winslow reflect the problems that incoming Loyalists encountered in resettling in Nova Scotia.

It is estimated that seventy-five to eighty thousand Loyalists left the United States during the war for England, Canada, the West Indies, and other parts of the British empire. Pamphlets of refugees like Joseph Galloway, which are reprinted here, reveal much about the views of the Loyalists who went to England. Some individuals remained men without a country, and lived out their days in London while dreaming about America. Others took up careers on the continent, as is evident in George E. Ellis' *Memoir of Sir Benjamin Thompson, Count Rumford*. Another major group—the United Empire Loyalists—whose story is presented in certain of these writings, settled in Canada and became the founding fathers of new communities.

The Loyalist Library includes also valuable primary source materials. Loyalist letters, pamphlets, and personal narratives help to shed light on the key question: Why did the American Tories remain loyal to their King? Prominent Loyalists like Daniel Leonard of Massachusetts and Joseph Galloway of Pennsylvania explain their political position in their writings. They tell us what they considered to be the proper relationship between colonies and mother country, the King and his subjects, and colonial governors and the American people. Until we view the Loyalists as men with "positive political ideas" and individuals capable of "creative statesmanship," a balanced interpretation of the Revolution will elude us, says one historian.

The Loyalist Library, then, is a combination of primary source documents and secondary materials. It includes private letters, diaries, and narratives, Tory histories and pamphlets, as well as scholarly books written on the subject. The collection makes available certain sources that were heretofore less accessible, and it should enable students to become more familiar with the Loyalist side of the story of the Revolution.

PREFACE

OTIS G. HAMMOND, who wrote extensively about New Hampshire's role in the Revolutionary era, turns his attention here to the New Hampshire Loyalists. The Loyalist movement in the colony appears to have been very weak. Political apathy was the rule instead. Hammond concludes that at most 200 men were guilty of or charged with "Royalist tendencies"—and that even some of them were falsely accused..

Many of the Loyalists, according to Hammond, were "passive Royalists." "[They] maintained a strict, dignified, and silent neutrality, watching the contest with disapproval, but obeying the laws established by the State in which they retained their abode, paying the taxes assessed on them, and observing a careful regard for the highly excited and nervous state of public opinion." Numbered among them were royal officeholders, "members of the oldest, best educated, wealthiest, and most aristocratic families," Anglican clergymen and their communicants, and professional men. Hammond suggests also a generation-gap interpretation, claiming that many Loyalists were older men "who did not easily change the opinions and attachments of long life under the Crown."

Religion proved to be one of the main reasons why men turned Loyalist. One of the two Anglican churches in the colony—Trinity Church in Claremont—was a center of

Loyalist activity. Writing about the Claremont congregation Hammond notes: "To these men, strong in their belief in a united church and state, any attack on the body politic of England was almost in the same degree an attack on the church." Claremont was also the location of a swamp called "Tory Hole"—a hiding place for Loyalists in a chain of rendez-vous extending from New York into Canada.

Portsmouth, however, turned out to be the major center for New Hampshire's Loyalists. One reason was that it was the colony's largest community. Hammond observes that fifteen members of the town's most respected and influential families were arrested in 1777 for suspicious activities, but twelve were soon· released under bond, with the warning that they were to say or do nothing that would be detrimental to the best interests of the United States. Portsmouth was also the site of the second Anglican church—Queen's Chapel. Hammond notes, however, that its rector, Arthur Browne, the father-in-law of Robert Rogers—a prominent Loyalist and leader of Rogers' Rangers—remained an "absolute neutral."

Hammond's study contains detailed information about New Hampshire's Loyalists—their place of residence, occupations, religious affiliations, and political sentiments. It supports the general conclusion among historians that New Hampshire was slow in joining her sister colonies during the imperial crisis, and that once committed the colony had relatively few Tories.

George Athan Billias
Clark University

TORIES OF NEW HAMPSHIRE

TORIES

OF

NEW HAMPSHIRE

IN THE

WAR OF THE REVOLUTION

OTIS GRANT HAMMOND

Superintendent of the New Hampshire Historical Society

CONCORD, N. H.
NEW HAMPSHIRE HISTORICAL SOCIETY
1917

THE TORIES OF NEW HAMPSHIRE.

BY OTIS G. HAMMOND.

The Word "Tory," although it has been variously modified by circumstances from its earliest use as applied to the outlawed Papists of Ireland in the reign of Charles II, down to its giving way to the present term, "Conservative," has always had a negative significance, an idea of opposition to political changes and a reverence for the existing order of government. To use a modern synonym, the Tories were always "stand-patters."

Since the Restoration, a Tory's political opponent has always been a Whig, the forefather of the Liberal of present-day English politics. The Whig was always the restless, ambitious, progressive element, eager for a change, without necessarily having established the fact that the change would be practical or beneficial to his party.

During the Revolution, and since in America, as might be expected in view of the victory of the opposition, the word "Tory" acquired a peculiarly ignominious meaning which did not pertain to its earlier use. It came by common consent to be used as almost synonymous with the word "traitor." Had the Tory party been victorious in the struggle the same significance would have been forced upon the word Whig.

The word "Tory" was applied indiscriminately to all who refused or failed to support the Revolutionary movement, regardless of their reasons for so doing, or of the degree of activity they displayed against that movement.

The Tories applied to themselves the name "Loyalist," a term respectable and admirable in its meaning, but not definite *per se*. A man may be loyal to anything to which he has once attached himself, his country, his church, his superior officer, or his wife. The Loyalists were loyal to their King. Those who rebelled against the Crown considered themselves loyal to their constitutional rights as

3

Englishmen, and to the new standards of government they had set up in order to maintain those rights.

On the other side the name "Whig," an old English political term, applied originally to the country party, as opposed to the Tory, the court or administration party, and the name "Patriot," as the colonist loved to call himself, are equally lacking in definite and accurate meaning as applied to those Americans who rose in rebellion against the unjust and burdensome demands of George III and his Parliament. The men of both sides considered themselves patriots, and the word is quite as applicable, in its true meaning, to one side as to the other. In this discussion I shall venture the use of the terms Royalist and Revolutionist as substitutes for the names we have inherited from our forefathers, substitutes more accurate in their significance and entirely free from the false interpretations of hatred and strife. A Royalist is one who maintains his loyalty to his King through the stress of rebellion. A Revolutionist is one who has risen in arms against a constituted authority and won.

In this present day we have no right to consider a man a Royalist unless we find in the official archives, or in contemporary private records of good authority, some evidence of his preference for the continuation of the Royal jurisdiction in America, or some evidence of his having suffered for such opinions. The fact that a man was suspected, harassed, arrested, or even imprisoned does not necessarily prove that he was a true Royalist, but proves only that he was so considered at that time by some people. Trials on these charges were not held before a court of law, but before the provincial committee of safety or some local committee, and there was one in every town. The judges in these cases were not versed in the law, and there were no rules of evidence. Witnesses were allowed to say what they pleased, and hearsay evidence was freely admitted.

Commitments to prison were made oftener on reasonable suspicion than on proven charges. But it is now too la' to appeal any of these cases or to review the evidence as comparatively little of it was ever recorded. In considering the whole class of Royalists in New Hampshire we must then, necessarily, include all who appear to have been under suspicion, bearing in mind the prejudices of the time, the excited state of the public mind, and the crude methods of trial by which the defendants were judged. Of about 200 suspected persons in New Hampshire only 76 were of sufficient guilt to be included in the proscription act, and to suffer the penalty of banishment, and against several of these there is no evidence on record except the fact that they had left the State.

We must not consider the entire body of Royalists in New Hampshire as actively engaged in opposing the measures of the Revolutionists. Many of them maintained a strict, dignified, and silent neutrality, watching the contest with disapproval, but obeying the laws established by the State in which they retained their abode, paying the taxes assessed upon them, and observing a careful regard for the highly excited and nervous state of public opinion. They were passive Royalists, and among their number we find many officials of the Royal government, members of the oldest, best educated, wealthiest, and most aristocratic families, clergymen of the Church of England and many of their communicants, men of the learned professions, and aged men who did not easily change the opinions and attachments of long life under the Crown. But harmless as their conduct was, these men did not escape the penalty of their convictions. With others more active they suffered prosecution by the authorities and persecution by unauthorized and irresponsible individuals. In this respect the war of the Revolution was no different from any other war. Non-combatants residing in the enemy's country never lead a peaceful, happy, or prosperous life, and a memory of this unjust feature of warfare still rankles in the minds of thousands, north and south, who suffered insult, abuse, and financial ruin in the great War of the Rebellion. It is the inevitable result of the high tension which is always produced by a conflict of arms, which sees things that are not, and magnifies things that are. The treatment the Royalists received in America, though in many cases unjust and severe, was only what might fairly have been expected, and what many others have suffered before and since in similar circumstances. It was only a normal price they had to pay for their unyielding principles, their minority, and their inability or failure to leave the field of action.

In March, 1776, Congress deemed it necessary to ascertain the extent of Royalism in the colonies, and recommended that a test be submitted to the people. It was considered that those who signed it could be depended upon to support the Revolutionary movement, and those who did not sign it were to be disarmed and so made for a time incapable of effective opposition. This pledge was called the Association Test, and the text was as follows:

"We, the Subscribers, do hereby solemnly engage and promise that we will to the utmost of our Power, at the Risque of our Lives and Fortunes, with Arms oppose the Hostile Proceedings of the British Fleets and Armies, against the United American Colonies."

By request of Congress this was presented for signature to all males above twenty-one years of age except lunatics, idiots, and negroes. Printed copies were sent to all the towns, and they were presented to the people for signature. Unfortunately not all the returns from New Hampshire towns have been preserved in our archives.

The nearest census was that of 1773. At that time there were 180 granted towns in the State, but many of them were unincorporated, unorganized, and even unsettled. The census of 1773 includes returns from 136 towns, and gives the province a population of 72,092, with several towns omitted. The returns of the census of 1786 are from 138 towns, the delinquents being far more numerous than in 1773, and a population of 95,452 is shown for the State. So that we may fairly assume the population of the colony in 1776 at 75,000, dwelling in about 150 settled or partly settled towns.

The 87 towns from which the Association Test returns

have been preserved in the archives represented a total of 50,682 of population, or 66 per cent. of the population of the colony at that time. These returns bear the signatures of 8,567 men, and the names of 781 who did not sign. One hundred and thirty-one of these refused because of religious scruples, conscience, or other reasons not hostile to the cause of the colonies, and 4 were reported absent, leaving 646, or 6.9 per cent. of possible signers, who refused to sign without apparent reason other than an unwillingness to support the war.

In Acworth, Antrim, Atkinson, Barnstead, Bow, Brookline, Canaan, Candia, Canterbury, Chester, Concord, Conway, Dublin, Effingham, Enfield, Gilsum, Lebanon, Lempster, Loudon, Manchester, Meredith, Newport, North Hampton, Peterborough, Piermont, Rindge, Rye, Seabrook, Sunapee, Surry, Wakefield, 31 towns, all signed.

In Danville, Kingston, and Northwood all but 19 signed, and these declined for reasons of conscience, and 5 of these were Danville and Northwood Quakers. In Kingston one man, James Carruth, a Scotchman, "Declines obliging himself to take up Arms against his Native Country but Declares he will neaver take up Arms against America, & is willing to bear his Proportion of the publick taxes with his Townsmen." One man, Moses Welch, "refuses to take up arms & pleads Conscience for an excuse." Twelve men "Appear to be fearful that the Signing of this Declaration would in some measure be an infringement on their Just Rights & Libertys but they Appear to be Friendly to their Country & Several of them have Ventured their lives in the American Cause & the 3 last named Persons are now in the Army."

Of those who refused to sign for reasons of religion or conscience 73 were Quakers, located in Danville 4, Kensington 15, Northwood 1, Rochester 22, Weare 31.

Other reasons for not signing are very interesting, amusing, some of them, and worthy of analysis.

In Bedford the Rev. John Houston declined "firstly Because he did not apprehend that the Honble committee

meant that ministers Should Take up arms as Being incon-
sistant with their Ministerial Charge, 2ndly Because he was
already confin'd to the County of Hillsborough, therefore he
thinks he Ought to be set at liberty before he Should Sign
the Sd obligation, 3rdly Because there is three men Belonging to his Family already Inlisted in the Continental army."

In Gilmanton, of 35 men refusing to sign, 21 state their
reasons as follows: "there being some scruples on our minds
We Cant Conscientiously sign it and we beg Leave to assign
our Reasons which are as follows, viz., we agree and Consent
to the Declaration of Independence on the British Crown,
and we are willing to pay our proportion to the support of
the United Colonies, but as to defend with arms, it is
against our Religious principles and pray we may be Ex-
cused."

In Kensington the selectmen, in returning the names
of those who would not sign, after making a list of 15 names,
said "So Far is Quakers as these two collums and What is to
Come your honours may Call What you please." Then
follow the names of five men who apparently did not stand
high in the estimation of the selectmen.

In Loudon all signed except "one or two that lived very
much out of the way." The failure to obtain these signatures was by the indolence of the selectmen by their own
confession.

In Newcastle, of the 4 who are returned as refusing to
sign, one, Richard Yeaton, Jr., is recorded as a soldier, and
was probably at that time absent in the service.

In Nottingham, of 25 non-signers, 10 are credited with
having advanced money to hire men to go to Crown Point.

In Richmond 12 men give as their reasons for not signing
that "We do not Believe that it is the Will of God to take
away the Lives of our fellow crators, not that We Come Out
Against the Congress or the Amarican Liberties, but When
Ever We are Convinct to the Contory We are Redy to join
our Amarican Brieathen to Defend by Arms Against the
Hostile Attempts of the British fleets and Armies."

In Sandown "Samuel Stevens did not Sign but is Since gon into the war."

The Test was not satisfactory to James Treadway of Canaan, nor were the ordinary rules of warfare severe enough to satiate his blood-thirsty patriotism. He signed, but imposed these conditions: "that no man who is taken a captive from the British forces be made an Officer or let be a Soldier in the Continental Army and 2^{ly} that Every American found & taken in armes against the United Colonies be immediately put to Death, and 3^{ly} that all & every of the British Troops that are Captivated by the Continental forces by sea or land, or any other way taken Shall be kept in Prison or Close Confinement, & 4^{ly} that Every Commanding Officer or a Soldier, or any Person or Persons employed in any business whatsoever in the Continental Forces, who is found and proved to be a Traitor to the United Colonies in America be put to Death Immediately."

Upon whom he imposed these conditions, or whom he expected to carry out his revised rules of war in order to secure his allegiance to the cause of independence does not appear.

Moses Flanders of South Hampton also signed on condition that the acts or advice of the Continental Congress relating to minute-men be complied with.

In the town of Temple the Association Test was construed literally as involving not only enlistment into the service, but extraordinary efforts in the field after such enlistment, and in town meeting the text of the document was so revised that the inhabitants might sign it without doing violence to their consciences. The selectmen said on their return of the Test, "We produced to the inhabitants of this Town in Town Meeting the Paper proposed by the Committee of Safety to be Sign^d by the Inhabitants of this Colony. Few, if any of the Inhabitants were willing to engage & promis as there proposed, to oppose by Arms to the utmost of their power the hostile Attempts of ye British Fleets & Armies— As this seem'd to the Inhabitants plainly to imply Something far more than any Common Enlistment into the Service, over engaging as soldiers directly & during the

Continuance of the war, as well as exerting ouer selves faithfully when engaged: this, at least, being within the Compass of our power. But it did not appear to the inhabitants prudent or Necessary for any, or in any Degree lawfull for all thus to engage. The Town directly adopted the Form of Association Sign^d on this paper which they and we hope expresses all Required by the general Congress."

The revised form adopted was thus:

"We the Subscribers, do hereby solemnly Profess our Intire willingness, at the Risque of our Lives and Fortunes, with Arms, to oppose the Hostile Attempts of the British Fleets, and Armies, against the United American Colonies, when Ever And to such A Degree as Such Attempts of Britain may Require." This was signed by all but three of those to whom it was presented.

Refusing to sign the Association Test did not, alone, make a man a Royalist, nor did the signing of it make him in fact a Revolutionist. The Association Test was promulgated for the purpose of ascertaining the sentiment of every man in the colonies who was qualified to bear arms. The declaration therein was not one of mere moral support to the cause of America, but was in its actual words a solemn promise to resist the power of Great Britain by force of arms; and the signer pledged his fortune and even his life in defense of American liberty. It was a powerful obligation, almost an enlistment into the armies of the United Colonies. Many who signed it never saw a moment's service in field or garrison, although they had sworn to take up arms to resist the invasion which afterwards occurred. Many who refused to sign it have left on record no evidence of opposition, by word or deed, to the establishment of an independent government. Some who signed it were afterwards convicted as Royalists, and suffered various penalties inflicted by duly authorized officers of the State, by irresponsible gatherings of the people, or by the malice of individuals. Some who refused to sign it were undoubted patriots, and supported the measures for carrying on the war to the extent of their moral and financial ability.

The Association Test was presented to young and old, able-bodied and infirm alike, the lame, the halt, and the blind, and was generally regarded in the light in which it was circulated, as a test of allegiance or opposition to the Revolutionary movement. Those who refused to sign it did so for various reasons; some because they honestly believed that the colonies had no just cause for resorting to the extremity of rebellion against the Crown; some because their love for the mother country and their reverence for English law and government caused them to look with horror upon any plan for disunion, or even any questioning of the justice and wisdom of Royal decrees; some because they read the Association Test literally, and were unable to perform its requirements, being either physically incapacitated for active service, or morally opposed to any act of war; some because they believed that, although the colonies had just cause for opposing the measures of the home government, a resort to war would lead only to sure defeat and an increased burden of taxation and oppression; some because of private pique and resentment of certain measures affecting their own personal welfare; some because of actual persecution by which they were afterwards driven into the British lines.

Those who signed the Test were also actuated by various motives. There can be no question that most of them did so from purely patriotic impulses, fully convinced that the attitude of Parliament towards the colonies, from the Stamp Act down to the Boston Port Bill, was unjust and oppressive, and that they were denied the natural political liberties accorded to Englishmen in every other part of the King's dominions, and constitutionally guaranteed to all the King's subjects wherever they might dwell. But there were those who signed for mercenary reasons, and paid the taxes levied on their property for carrying on the war to the end that they might preserve their estates from the ruin which was more or less certain to be visited upon the hated minority. There were also those who yielded to threats, and petty but continued and determined annoyances, which impressed their minds with the belief that what was then but an annoyance was the forerunner of certain disaster.

I find record evidence of guilt or suspicion of Royalist tendencies against about 200 men in New Hampshire. Many of these were prosecuted on suspicion founded on evidence of the most flimsy texture, and the formal charges brought against them were such as counterfeiting, or attempting to circulate counterfeit paper money, trying to spread small pox, or saying things, which spoken carelessly or in jest, gave their neighbors a long sought opportunity of revenge, or of posing before the authorities as zealous advocates of liberty. So that these figures do not represent the actual number of Royalists in New Hampshire, but the number of those who were, by any possible pretext, brought under official suspicion.

There was undoubtedly much counterfeiting in all the colonies, but there is no evidence that there was any concerted or organized attempt at this practice among the Royalists, although individually they did, as Gen. Sullivan says, disparage the value of colonial bills of credit in comparison with British or Spanish gold. The paper money of the Revolutionary period was crude in design, of many different forms, each colony issuing its own series, and the Federal government still other series, and the business of counterfeiting was extremely easy and profitable. As the war progressed paper money became so plentiful as to be enormously depreciated from its face value in specie, and in the Continental Army depreciation pay rolls were made up every year for paying to the soldiers the lost value of their wages. In these circumstances it is hardly fair to charge the Royalists with the responsibility for all the counterfeiting that was perpetrated in the colonies. As to the accusation that they attempted to spread the small pox in order to lessen the fighting force against Great Britain, it is too absurd and lacking in proof to be worth a moment's consideration. This was a hallucination natural to the time when small pox was one of the most dreaded diseases of a military camp. Vaccination had not been discovered, but inoculation with true small pox was extensively practised with the object of gaining immunity by having the disease in a degree somewhat modified from the normal by medical care, and, if possible, under hospital conditions, from the beginning.

In May, 1775, Philip Bailey, James McMaster, and Thomas Achincloss, all of Portsmouth, were persuaded to sign recantations like this:

"Whereas, I the subscriber, have, for a long series of time, both done and said many things that I am sensible has proved of great disadvantage to this Town, and the Continent in general; and am now determined by my future conduct to convince the publick that I will risk my life and interest in defense of the constitutional privileges of this Continent, and humbly ask the forgiveness of my friends and the Country in general for my past conduct." (Am. Arch., 4th ser., v. 2, p. 552.)

May 15, 1775, the town of Portsmouth passed a vote to support the local committee of safety, and giving that committee sole jurisdiction over any obnoxious persons who might flee to that town for asylum; and, in view of the impending scarcity of provisions, they advised the inhabitants to refrain from purchasing any lamb that might be killed before the first day of August, and from killing any lambs before that date; and recommended the use of fresh fish twice a week at least. (7 N. H. State Papers, 467.)

Gen. John Sullivan, in a letter to Gen. Washington dated Oct. 29, 1775, in regard to the defences of Portsmouth harbor, speaks his mind in regard to the Royalists of that locality. He says:

"That infernal crew of Tories, who have laughed at the Congress, despised the friends to liberty, endeavoured to prevent fortifying this harbour, and strove to hurt the credit of the Continental money, and are yet endeavouring it, walk the streets here with impunity, and will, with a sneer, tell the people in the streets that all our liberty-poles will soon be converted into gallows. I must entreat your

Excellency to give some directions what to do with those persons, as I am fully convinced that, if an engagement was to happen, they would, with their own hands, set fire to the town, expecting a reward from the Ministry for such hellish service. Some who have for a long time employed themselves in ridiculing and discouraging those who were endeavouring to save the Town, have now turned upon me and are now flying from one street to another, proclaiming that you gave me no authority or license to take ships to secure the entrance of the harbor, or did anything more than send me here to see the Town reduced to ashes if our enemies thought proper. Sir, I shall await your directions respecting those villians, and see that they are strictly complied with by your Excellency's most obedient servant.

J. S."

(Am. Archives, 4th ser. v. 3, p. 1252.)

To which Gen. Washington replied more temperately Nov. 12, 1775:

"I therefore desire that you will delay no time in causing the seizure of every officer of Government at Portsmouth who have given pregnant proofs of their unfriendly disposition to the cause we are engaged in; and when you have seized them, take the opinion of the Provincial Congress or Committee of Safety in what manner to dispose of them in that Government. I do not mean that they should be kept in close confinement. If either of those bodies should incline to send them to any of the interior Towns, upon their parole not to leave them till released, it will meet with my concurrence.

"For the present, I avoid giving you the like order in respect to the Tories in Portsmouth, but the day is not far off when they will meet with this or a worse fate, if there is not considerable reformation in their conduct. Of this they may be assured."

In order to accurately ascertain the public sentiment in regard to the Royalists we must go to some contemporary record to which the public had free access for the registration of its opinions. There is no such record but the newspapers.

The New Hampshire Gazette, founded at Portsmouth in 1756, and still issued weekly, now the oldest newspaper of continuous publication in the United States, gives us a fair idea of the popular estimate of the Tory. A few extracts are well worth repeating.

In the issue of Sept. 21, 1776, is an article signed "Namora," a name which is easily seen to be "A Roman" spelled backwards. Namora says:

"It's astonishing to see daily, the insults offered by the Tories, and unnoticed by the Committee, in a more particular manner, since the news of the skirmish on Long Island; on the first report, they had their meeting and a dinner provided to congratulate each other on the importance of the day; and, if common fame speaks truth, they have their particular toasts on such occasions; their significant nods and smiles at each other as they pass by, and in their very countenances it is as plain to be seen as the sun in its meridian. They have the effrontery to assert that it is much worse than reported; that it's so bad that the sons of Liberty are afraid to let it be known, least the people should be discouraged. Is not this intollerable? It's a matter of fact that they have the first news on every event, and that they propagate every intelligence they receive, taking care to calculate it, so as to serve their own turn; it's beyond a matter of doubt that they keep up a secret correspondence thro' the colonies in order to comfort one another, to keep up their sinking spirits, and to propagate falsehoods."

* * *

The following sarcastic reply to Namora was found in the hallway of the Gazette office, and the editor printed it the following week as a curiosity:

"Well done Namora, you talk sence, you preach liberty, real genuine liberty, downright, alamode liberty, by G-d! I must observe, however, that I was at first a good deal alarmed on discovering your design of abolishing looks and nods, those dear conveyors of our secret meaning; but when I found you only meant significant ones, and that out of the abundance of your great goodness and impartiality you had confined it to tories, I was immediately reconcil'd to it, and discovered, by the help of certain political microscopic glasses, that it tended to the public good.

"It is, indeed, no less than alarming, that these damn'd tories have the impudence to meet, speak, eat, and drink together as other men do; yea, they have the effrontery, in open violation of the laws both of God and man, to cast at each other, as they pass, their significant looks and nods; intolerable! and still they go unnoticed by the committee; amazing! 'Tis a disgrace to the state to allow of such significant looks and nods, and if the legislative body of these states have not, in their great wisdom, already provided a punishment adequate to the diabolical nature of so black a crime (which hardly admits of a doubt), I think the honorable committee of this town, if they desire that the trumpet of fame should sound their praises to after ages, cannot have a fairer opportunity of immortallizing their names than by enacting laws against such treasonable and unheard of practices; which would at once discover their patriotic zeal for their country, their wise and god-like penetration into the nature and cause of things, and their unerring knowledge of mankind, who carry on daily the most villainous conspiracies in no other language than looks and nods; O, most shocking! What dreadful ills have not been done by noding? I humbly think a significant look ought to be punished by a burning out of the optics, and a nod by severing off the offender's head from the unoffending body; this would be going justly and regularly to work; it would be removing causes, as the surest way to prevent effects.

"And now, Mr. Printer, in case you or any of your readers, should be so abandoned to toryism, or so full of that brutish feeling, humanity, as to think the above hints toward enacting laws for the regulation of tories are too severe, even for that infernal set of beings; or, if either of you should be so unwise or unacquainted with the unbounded power of committees, as to imagine that (though that same cumbersome feeling above mentioned, could be stifled) yet these laws are in their nature chimerical, wild, and not

reducible to practice, and consequently that my worthy
friend Namora (who to tell you the truth is no other than
a double-headed monster, bred behind a Spring hill counter)
and myself are wicked, designing devils, & foolish withall,
I hereby certify & declare to all men, that tho' I may be a
foolish devil, yet, I am neither a wicked or designing one,
and that these two last epithets, with all the detestable
ideas attending them, are only applied to my double-headed
friend; this being only a kind of explanatory supplement to
this piece, I am

(signed)   What you will"

In the Gazette of Jan. 14, 1777, appeared another expres-
sion of opinion entitled
"To the Public.
"Is it not amazing, astonishing to every thinking mind
at this Period, when nothing but Rapine and Murder can
Satiate the Lust of those Infernal Devils sent among us
by the Infamous Tyrant of Britain, that there can still be
found a single Person who yet retains that odious name of a
Tory, when they see (notwithstanding their much boasted
Loyalty) their wives & Daughters are not exempt from the
Ravaging Cruelties of those Wretches, any more than those
of the Rebels (so called); by which Treatment alone, (though
void of all Principle) one might reasonably expect it would
exasperate and Excite them to such a degree of Resentment
and Revenge, that all their pretended Loyalty would in-
stantly vanish, and with Heart and Hand join their much
Injured Country-men in sheathing their Swords in the
Breasts of such Brutal Animals; which would afford much
more consolation to a noble Mind than to sit down, tamely
submitting to the Murderous Decrees issued by a vile, Des-
potic Tyrant, to be executed by the very dregs of H-ll.
Oh! it makes my very blood boil with Indignation at the
thoughts of such horrid Deeds, and much more when I
reflect that there are many such shameful Wretches among
us at this late Hour, that would sell their God, their Country,
their Wives, their Children, and all that is near and dear to

them. Pray, what is the reward due to such Monsters?
Do they deserve the Lenity shown them by their Townsmen?
Don't they rather deserve the halter? Nay, is not even
that too good for them? Can any infliction of Punishment
(though ever so severe) be called too Cruel? Upon the
whole, what ought to be done in order to Rid us of such
Vermin? Suppose I should suggest a mode, and that is to
provide some kind of a Bark, and, after putting on board
some Provisions, Set them a Drift, & make it death for any
of them ever to land on any Part of the American Shore
that is Inhabited by Freemen, which in my opinion would
be the best and most effectual method, and much milder
than such Slaves could reasonably expect.

(Signed)   An Enemy to Tories."

May 31, 1777, the Gazette editorially suggested that
they be "taken up, sent and kept under a Strong Guard
(at their own expense, so far as their Estates will go), in
some of the New Townships, there to continue during the
War."

Feb. 18, 1777, the Gazette printed

"A Whisper to the Folks called Tories.

" As you have given Bonds not to disturb the Peace of
the Town, nor do anything directly or indirectly against
the American Cause, would advise, that you keep in your
own Houses as much as possible, and not assemble together
in the Street or elsewhere in too great a number, as that
will be look'd upon as an indirect Method taken against
the public Good, and subject your Persons to insults. It
would also be prudent for those who desire to preserve
the Name of staunch Whigs, not to join their Assemblies
so frequently in the open Streets, as that gives a sanction
to their evil Doings. The Court has acquited them on
conditions, therefore pass them with silent contempt, and
let their own guilty reflections be their Punishment. It
would also be proper that whifling Whigs should be distinguished, and assemble together, as their mixing with either
of the above is taking an unfair Advantage, and conse-

quently brings a Reflection on both Parties, as they must be considered by the Public a Species beneath the Notice of either Class."

July 19, 1777, the House of Representatives appointed a committee to report some method for taking firearms from such persons in the State as refused to take up arms against the enemies of the American States. The same day the committee recommended that the colonels of the several regiments of militia be empowered to disarm the disaffected persons, and that the arms so taken be appraised by two disinterested men, and be paid for unless returned. The recommendation was adopted, but we find no record of further action on this plan, although here and there a few Royalists were disarmed by local committees of safety.

A curious incident of the time is the suspicion of the Quakers. Aug. 28, 1777, the Federal Congress stated that there was reason to believe that Quakers in different States were carrying on a treasonable correspondence, and recommended that the States investigate the matter by seizing and examining their records and papers, and that any documents of a political nature so found be forwarded to Congress. November 8 following the New Hampshire House of Representatives appointed a committee to apply to clerks of the Quaker societies in Dover, Hampton Falls, Seabrook, Brentwood, Weare, and other towns for the privilege of examining their records, and gave the committee power to break and enter in case access was refused. There is no evidence on record that any incriminating documents were found among the Quakers of New Hampshire.

Officially it was intended from the beginning that there should be no persecution of Royalists, and no action of any kind against them except by due process of law. June 18, 1776, the Federal Congress resolved "that no man in these colonies charged with being a Tory, or unfriendly to the cause of American liberty, be injured in his person or property, or in any manner whatever disturbed, unless the proceeding against him be founded on an order of this Congress, or the assembly, convention, council, or committee of safety of the colony, or committee of inspection and observation of the district where he resides; provided that this resolution shall not prevent the apprehending any person found in the commission of some act destructive of American liberty, or justly suspected of a design to commit such act, and intending to escape, and bringing such person before proper authority for examination and trial."

January 17, 1777, the New Hampshire House of Representatives passed a resolution giving all disaffected persons three months in which to leave the State unmolested, with their families and effects, with the privilege of selling their property before departure; and requiring them to register their intentions with the selectmen of their respective towns thirty days before leaving; and these registrations were to be transmitted to the Secretary of State. This did not become operative as law, the Council neglecting to concur, but it is valuable as showing the fair and reasonable intentions of the representative body of the people. The same day the Council passed an act defining treason and misprision of treason, and providing a penalty of death without benefit of clergy; and an act for punishing lesser offences of a treasonable nature, such as discouraging enlistments, speaking against the cause of the States, and spreading false reports.

June 19, 1777, an act was passed authorizing the Committee of Safety to issue warrants to sheriffs, deputy-sheriffs, or any other person, for the commitment to jail of "any person whom the said Committee of Safety shall deem the Safety of the Common Wealth requires should be restrained of his personal Liberty, or whose Enlargement within this state is dangerous thereto," there to remain without bail until discharged by order of the committee or the General Court; and the committee was given power of examination and trial in such cases.

November 29 an act was passed to prevent the transfer of property by persons apprehended on suspicion, and for securing the lands of those who had gone over to the enemy, or might do so, and of those who resided in Great Britain.

These acts were all preliminary, and show the gradual development of a hostile sentiment in the legislature and among the people.

The Proscription Act, or act of banishment, was passed Nov. 19, 1778, and bore the title "An act to prevent the return to this state of certain persons therein named, and of others who have left or shall leave this state, or either of the United States of America, and have joined or shall join the enemies thereof." Seventy-six men are named in the act, first of whom was Gov. John Wentworth, and they are described as having left this State and joined the enemies thereof, "thereby not only basely deserting the cause of liberty and depriving these states of their personal services at a time when they ought to have afforded their utmost assistance in defending the same against the invasions of a cruel enemy, but abetting the cause of tyranny, and manifesting an enimical disposition to said states, and a design to aid the enemies thereof in their wicked purposes."

An analysis of this list of 76 outlawed Royalists is interesting, especially if we may consider it as fairly representative of the whole body of Royalists in New Hampshire, fairly indicative of the classes and the proportions of each that we may find in the entire number. In this list we find 30 "Esquires" or gentlemen (using social distinctions of that time rather than this), 1 military officer, 5 mariners, 4 physicians, 8 merchants, 5 traders, 19 yeomen or farmers, 1 ropemaker, 1 post-rider, 1 printer, and 1 clerk or minister. Thirty-three of these were citizens of Portsmouth; Londonderry and Dunbarton had 6 each, Keene 5, Charlestown 4, Hollis 3, Newmarket, Amherst, Alstead and Hinsdale, 4 each, and Pembroke, Exeter, Concord, Merrimack, New Ipswich, Francestown, Peterborough, Nelson, Winchester, Rindge, and Claremont 1 each.

The geographical distribution covers very nearly the whole of the State that was under settlement at that time, and seems to defy the application of any particular theory of locality. It extended from the Atlantic Ocean to the Connecticut River, and from the Massachusetts line to

Claremont on the north. There was no large number in any one town except Portsmouth, which held nearly half the entire list. This fact was perfectly natural to the place which had been the seat of the Royal government for nearly a century. From a social point of view it will be noticed that 30 of the 76 belonged to the class of gentlemen, and 5 others were of the learned professions. The penalty provided in the act for a voluntary return to the State was for a first offense transportation to British territory, and for a second offense death.

The Confiscation Act followed eight days later, or Nov. 28, 1778, and in it were named 25 of those included in the Proscription Act, and three others not previously mentioned. They were described as men who "have, since the commencement of hostilities between Great Britain and the United States of America, left this and the other United States, and gone over to and joined the enemys thereof, and have, to the utmost of their power, aided, abetted, and assisted the said enemys in their cruel designs of wresting from the good people of said states their Libertys, civil and religious, and of taking from them their property, and converting the same to the use of their said enemys." All their property in New Hampshire was declared forfeited to the use of the State.

It will be noticed that the Proscription Act banished those who had left the state of their abode and joined the enemy, whether in the United Colonies or elsewhere; but the Confiscation Act seized the estates of those only who had departed from the country, sought refuge on British soil, and become perniciously active in opposition to the Revolutionary government. This will account for the difference in numbers affected by those respective acts.

Belknap says "In these acts no distinction was made between those persons who had withdrawn themselves from the state by a sense of their duty; those who were, in fact, British subjects, but occasionally resident here; those who had absconded through timidity; and those who had committed crimes against express law, and had fled from justice.

No conditional offer of pardon was made; no time was allowed for any to return and enter into the service of the country; but the whole were put indiscriminately into one black-list, and stigmatised as having basely deserted the cause of liberty and manifested a disposition inimical to the State, and a design to aid its enemies in their wicked purposes."

Confiscated estates aggregated a large sum in original value, but were greatly diminished by a period of bad management and neglect while in the hands of trustees. These values, like all others, were also affected by the almost ruinous depreciation of paper money, and the net income to the State from all confiscated property was very small.

It is not now necessary to argue the apparent conflict of these laws with the constitutional principle that no part of a man's property shall be taken from him without his consent, or due process of law. The constitution of 1776, which was in effect at the time of the passage of these laws, was a temporary enactment, intended, as stated in the preamble, to continue only "during the present unhappy and unnatural contest with Great Britain." It was a mere skeleton of a form of government, and it stood on a preamble and not a bill of rights. Government under it was provisional, and there was no constitutional government in New Hampshire until June, 1784, when our permanent constitution went into operation.

In his opinion in Dow v. Railroad, 67 N. H. 1, Judge Doe says: "Under the non-legislative reign of Parliament, and the pre-constitutional government of this State, there was no limit of governmental power to be decided or considered by the court. The acts of banishment and confiscation, passed and enforced by the provisional government of the Revolution, were as valid as the habeas corpus act." There was, then, no bar to the passage and execution of these laws by a government whose power had no constitutional limitations, but the act of confiscation was not in accord with the principle of the inviolability of private property which the fathers wished to embody in the constitution adopted in 1783; and at that time these acts were in force, and many confiscated estates were still in the process of settlement by the courts. In order, therefore, to re-affirm, establish, and definitely constitutionalize these acts, it was provided in the constitution that "nothing herein contained, when compared with the twenty-third article in the bill of rights [retroactive legislation], shall be construed to affect the laws already made respecting the persons or estates of absentees." This subject has been discussed by the court in Opinion of the Justices, 66 N. H. 629; Orr v. Quimby, 54 N. H. 591; Dow v. Railroad, 67 N. H. 1; State v. Express Co., 60 N. H. 219, and in other cases.

In 1777 the air was full of tales of Royalist plots in various parts of the State for doing all sorts of monstrous things. The Committee of Safety, writing to the delegates in Congress May 10, announced the discovery of several combinations in Hillsborough and Rockingham counties and the western parts of Massachusetts; a plan for organizing, arming, and joining the enemy; a hogshead of entrenching tools hidden under a barn in Hollis; and unusually large supplies of liquors, provisions, and arms in the vicinity of Groton, Massachusetts. The committee adds "Interesting Matters are opening, and it is probable that all our Gaols will soon be filled with these more than monsters in the Shape of men, who would wreck there Native Country in hopes to share some of the Plunder."

In January, 1777, on the occasion of sending some prisoners of war to Rhode Island, Timothy Walker, Jr., of Concord wrote to Col. Nicholas Gilman warning him that it was "vehemently suspected that our Tory Gentry in this part of the Country" were designing to send information to Howe's army by the prisoners. The Committee of Safety instructed Capt. John Haven, in command of the guard, to search the prisoners with the utmost care, and after examination to allow no man to address or approach them before embarkation.

In September the Committee of Safety in Plymouth reported the discovery of a suspected Royalist meeting.

They said "The Place and some Persons being Suspected,
a Secret Spy was Sent out in order to make Discovery, who
upon Return Reports That at & near the House of Brion
Sweeneys Northerly of Great Squam Pond in the Town of
Newholderness (a place very remote from any other humane
Settlement) was discovered Sundry Persons who by their
number & Dress did not appear to be the proper Inhabitants
of that place (no man in that family being Grown up but
Sweeny himself)."

In Claremont were a considerable number of genuine
Royalists, men who sincerely believed the colonies were
wrong, and who were willing to aid the King's forces to the
extent of their ability, even at some risk of discovery and
its well-known consequences. There never was in New
Hampshire any organization of Royalists, either for the
purpose of armed resistance to the Revolutionists, or for
giving indirect aid to the Crown. In some States, however,
notably New York, and consequently Vermont, because of
the powerful New York influences which prevailed through
all the territory between the Connecticut and the Hudson
Rivers, the Royalists were numerous and strong enough
to organize in various ways and for various purposes.
Claremont may have been affected by a combination of
two circumstances, proximity to a locality in which Royalists were bold, separated only by the span of the river, and
the existence within its borders of an organized parish of
the Church of England, whose members, though in the
minority, were active and ardent in their support of the
little church they had planted so far up in the frontier wilderness. To these men, strong in their belief in a united
church and state, any attack on the body politic of England
was almost in the same degree an attack on the church.

There was in Claremont a hiding place for Royalists,
one of a chain of rendezvous extending from New York to
Canada. It was known as Tory Hole, and was protected
on three sides by a swamp covered by a thick growth of
alders, and on the fourth side by a steep bank about 30
feet high. Here meetings were held in safety for a long

time, and travellers were sheltered and fed and passed on their journey. The existence of such a resort was long suspected by the Revolutionary party, but it was not discovered until late in the year 1780. Two men who were found there escaped by swimming across the Connecticut River and taking refuge on the top of Ascutney Mountain, where they were captured while asleep; and, being armed, were held as prisoners of war, sent to Boston, and afterwards exchanged.

In December, 1775, twenty-five men of Claremont were brought before a joint committee of safety from the towns of Claremont, Hanover, Lebanon and Cornish for examination, being suspected of Royalism. Among them were Rev. Ranna Cossitt, rector of the church, and Samuel Cole, schoolmaster and catechist under him, and most of the others were members of Mr. Cossitt's church. Mr. Cossitt, on examination, said "I believe the American Colonies, in their dispute with Great Britain, which has now come to blood, are unjust, but will not take up arms either against the King or country, as my office and circumstances are such that I am not obliged thereto. I mean to be on the side of the administration, and I had as leave any person should call me a damned Tory as not, and take it as an affront if people don't call me a Tory, for I verily believe the British troops will overcome by the greatness of their power and justice of their cause."

The joint committee disarmed all the persons examined, and recommended to the Provincial Congress that Capt. Benjamin Sumner, Samuel Cole, and Rev. Ranna Cossitt, as chief advisers and dictators, be placed in confinement. They were brought to trial in Charlestown April 10, 1776, and were sentenced to be confined to the town limits of Claremont until the close of the war unless they promised good behavior, Capt. Sumner being required to give bonds instead of promises for his release. They were forbidden to be seen together except at public worship, but Mr. Cossitt was allowed such liberty as was necessary for the performance of his ministerial office in preaching, baptizing, and visiting the sick.

Col. John Peters wrote from Quebec July 20, 1778, to his brother, Rev. Samuel Peters, in London, as follows:

"Rev. Dr. Wheelock, President of Dartmouth College in New Hampshire, in conjunction with Deacon Bayley, Mr. Morey, and Mr. Hurd, all justices of the peace, put an end to the Church of England in this state so early as 1775. They seized me, Capt. Peters, and all the judges of Cumberland and Gloucester, the Rev. Mr. Cossitt and Mr. Cole, and all the church people for 200 miles up the river and confined us in close gaols, after beating and drawing us through water and mud. Here we lay some time, and were to continue in prison until we abjured the King and signed the league and covenant. Many died, one of which was Capt. Peter's son. We were removed from the gaol and confined in private houses at our own expense. Capt. Peters and myself were guarded by twelve rebel soldiers while sick in bed, and we paid dearly for this honor; and others fared in like manner. I soon recovered from my indisposition, and took the first opportunity and fled to Canada, leaving Cossitt, Cole, Peters, Willis, Porter, Sumner, Paptin, etc., in close confinement where they had misery, insults, and sickness enough. My flight was in 1776, since which my family arrived at Montreal, and inform me that many prisoners died; that Capt. Peters had been tried by court martial and ordered to be shot for refusing to lead his company against the King's troops. He was afterwards reprieved but still in gaol, and that he was ruined both in health and property; that Cossitt and Cole were alive when they came away, but were under confinement, and had more insults than any of the loyalists, because they had been servants of the Society[1], which, under pretense (as the rebels say) of propagating religion, had propagated loyalty, in opposition to the liberties of America."

Mr. Cossitt himself wrote from New York June 6, 1779, to the Secretary of the Society for the Propagation of the

[1] Society for the Propagation of the Gospel in Foreign Parts.

Gospel: "I arrived in this city last Sunday by permission, with a flag, and am to return in a few days. I trust the Society cannot be unacquainted with the persecution the loyalists have endured in New England. I have been, by the committee, confined as a prisoner in the town of Claremont ever since the 12th of April, 1775, yet God has preserved my life from the people. I have constantly kept up public service, without any omissions, for the King and royal family, and likewise made use of the prayer for the high court of parliament, and the prayer to be used in time of war and tumults; have administered the Lord's Supper on every first Sunday in the month, except two Sundays that we could not procure any wine. The numbers of my parishoners and communicants in Claremont are increased, but I have been cruelly distressed with fines for refusing entirely to fight against the King. In sundry places where I used to officiate, the church people are all dwindled away. Some have fled to the King's army for protection, some were banished, and many died."

Mr. Cossitt remained at his post in Claremont until 1785, when he was sent as a missionary by the Society for the Propagation of the Gospel to Sidney, Cape Breton. He died there in 1815.

Rev. Dr. Hubbard, sometime rector of Trinity church, Claremont, in his centennial address of 1871, said

"We can hardly estimate aright at this distant day, and in the midst of circumstances so greatly changed, the position in which churchmen found themselves at the breaking out of the Revolutionary war. The period of religious toleration had not arrived, and the spirit of the ancient contests which had raged for centuries in the Old World, and in a measure spent their force, was here revived in all its intense bigotry and malignity. It was not the fear of such men as Samuel Cole and Ranna Cossitt, in a civil point of view, that led to their cruel persecution and abuse. Doubtless they were loyal to the government, and most warmly attached to the Church of England. But they were peaceable, law-abiding men. There was no treachery or sedition in them. Their own principles taught them to obey the powers that be. While the great struggle was going on they could not be hired or driven to take up arms against the King; neither would they take up arms, nor plot nor conspire against the lives and happiness of their fellow-citizens. They desired to remain quiet and await the decision of Providence. And when that decision came, if it were adverse to their hopes, they would be as faithful and obedient to the new government as they had been to the old."

The only other Protestant Episcopal Church in New Hampshire at this time was Queen's Chapel of Portsmouth, now called St. John's church. Its rector was Rev. Arthur Browne, a faithful and beloved priest and a man of spotless character. His attitude during the war was that of an absolute neutral. There is no record of any charge or suspicion against him. His son-in-law, however, Major Robert Rogers, commander of Rogers's Rangers in the French and Indian wars, was one of the most active Royalists, as well as one of the most famous soldiers of New England.

In January, 1777, fifteen citizens of Portsmouth were arrested by the town committee of safety on suspicion, and sent to the state committee at Exeter under guard. Among them were James Sheafe, Jonathan Warner, Peter and John Peirce, Isaac Rindge, and Nathaniel Treadwell, members of some of the most respected and influential families of Portsmouth in the days of the province. Among them, also, was John Stavers, keeper of the Earl of Halifax inn, a tavern which had been a favorite resort of the officers of the provincial government and of travellers from England. The place was naturally held in suspicion by the Sons of Liberty, and was once raided and nearly reduced to ruins. It was commonly thought that Royalist meetings were held there, and many threats were made against the house and its keeper. It is quite probable that these fifteen suspected persons, who seem to have been all gathered in at once, and among whom was the inn-keeper himself, were in attendance upon one of these meetings when arrested. Twelve of them were released under bonds of £500 each "not to say or do anything directly or Indirectly in anywise contrary or in Opposition to the American Cause now contending for, * * * or the United States of America for & during yᵉ Term of one year next coming, and further advise that they be very careful and cautious in these times of jealousy & danger, in giving any occasion of mistrust to any person Whatsomever of their dissatisfaction to the common cause. The Committee likewise recommend that People of every rank and denomination in this State be careful in detecting all persons speaking or conspiring against this or any of the United American States, and cause them to be prosecuted according to the Laws made & published for that purpose."

So many Royalists were committed to jail that an understanding of the entire subject cannot be complete without a knowledge of the character of the places in which they were confined. Each county had its jail, and Rockingham had two, one at Portsmouth, old, insecure, and not much used, and one at Exeter. The records preserve to our use a very good description of the Hillsborough county jail at Amherst, second only to that at Exeter in importance during the Revolution. Probably the other jails did not greatly differ from this in the main points of construction.

Built in 1772, it was 34 feet long, 26 feet wide, and 17 feet high, divided into two stories, probably 9 feet and 8 feet respectively. There were four rooms for the prisoners, each 11 feet square, two on each floor, but the jail-keeper's rooms were 14 feet long. The entry was 7 feet wide, opening into the jailer's apartments on one side, and the prisoner's quarters on the other. There was no cellar except under the end of the building occupied by the jailer. The posts, sills, and plates were of white oak, and the rest of the timber was chestnut, and the appropriation for the entire work was £200. The fence was 8 feet high, well spiked, and stood 10 feet from the building on all sides. The new jail was occupied in October of the same year, and at the same time an addition 18 feet in length was ordered to be built

on the jailer's end of the building.   On the 5th of November
a stove for use in the prison was voted by the court of
general sessions.   Later in the month the sheriff protested
that the jail was not secure, and it was ordered that the
prisoners' rooms be lathed and plastered, and that iron
bars, 3 inches apart, be set in the window of the lower north
room.   But laths and plaster were not effective in prevent-
ing escapes, and in August, 1773, two good locks and window
shutters for the same room were provided.   Joseph Kelley,
who had escaped once and threatened to do so again, was
put in chains.   In November even the doors had to be
fastened, and two locks and a padlock were ordered; the
fence, also, was insufficient, and the court ordered it to be
built 12 feet high and moved to 20 feet from the west and
north sides of the building.   Even this failed to prevent com-
munication with the prisoners from the outside.   In December, 1774, the sheriff went to the court in despair, and
represented that his locks and hinges were all broken, many
of the doors smashed, and that a large hole was cut through
the floor in the north room, and that all his prisoners were
gone.   The court responded with orders for the repair of the
building in the best and strongest possible manner, but
two years later, fourteen New York Royalists confined there
broke jail and escaped in one night.

In 1777, statements being made to the Committee of
Safety that the prisoners in Exeter jail had become very
sickly on account of bad air, the keeper of the jail, Capt.
Simeon Ladd, was instructed July 12 to permit the prisoners, one half the number at a time, to come out of close
confinement into the two front chambers and to remain
there under double guard from 6 o'clock in the morning until
6 o'clock in the afternoon.   A fire was allowed in the lower
jail from Dec. 13, 1777, to May 10, 1778, and the allowance
of wood was half a cord a week.   Apparently no fire was
kept on the second floor.   The following winter, however,
the committee was more merciful, and allowed fires both
up-stairs and down, and ordered them to be lighted as early
as Nov. 4.   Complaints from the prisoners of sickness on

account of foul air, unsanitary conditions, and vermin were very numerous.

The number of Royalists actually confined in prison was far exceeded by those sentenced to certain limitations. The common penalty in the less serious cases was confinement to the bounds of the town in which the defendant lived. Sometimes this restriction was enlarged to include an adjoining town or two, and occasionally the whole county; and some were forbidden to leave their estates except to attend public worship.

The first man in New Hampshire to suffer for his suspected Royalist tendencies was Benjamin Thompson of Concord, afterwards Count Rumford, who was driven from his natural allegiance to the colonies to seek protection within the British lines by continued unreasonable persecution, inspired and promoted by private jealousy and malice. Mr. Thompson had come from Woburn, Massachusetts, his native town, to Concord, New Hampshire, in 1772 to teach school. He had not a college education, but was possessed of a natural love for art, music, and especially for natural science. Before he had been in Concord six months he married Sarah, widow of Benjamin Rolfe and daughter of Rev. Timothy Walker, a woman of many charms, for she had youth, beauty, family, and the largest and finest estate in town. Immediately after his marriage he became acquainted with Gov. Wentworth, and found in him a man of charming manners, culture, wealth, and a taste for science which enabled them at once to meet on common ground. Mr. Thompson's errand to the Governor was to propose a survey of the White Mountains, and to his great delight the Governor not only thought well of the plan but offered the loan of some valuable instruments and books he had in his house at Wolfeborough, and proposed to go with the party himself if public business should allow. It is not strange that such flattering interest and attentions from the Royal Governor to the boy, for he was then only 20 years old, secured his enthusiastic and devoted admiration. The Governor's friendship was further manifested in 1773, when he gave Mr. Thompson a major's commission in a regiment of militia, and so placed him in a position of command over many officers and men of twice his age, and infinitely his superior in military knowledge and experience. It is a fair assumption that at his age his mind was fully occupied with his recent triumphs, his marriage and social position, his friendship with the Governor, and his military rank, all accomplished within about a year, to the exclusion of public affairs, in which he had never participated nor shown any particular interest. He did not see the intensity of the Revolutionary feeling among the people about him, nor was his knowledge of and experience with human nature sufficient to show him the normal result of an inordinate social attachment to the chief executive officer of an unpopular government. The jealousy and suspicion thus aroused were probably the primary cause of the hostile acts which soon followed. There was another contributing cause, but it was not of sufficient importance to have caused him more than the temporary inconvenience which a hundred others suffered under unjust suspicions which were soon cleared away. After his marriage Major Thompson became, of necessity, a farmer, and employed among others two men who afterwards proved to be deserters from the British army, desirous of returning to their duties but restrained by fear of the penalties for their crime. They were sent back to Boston by Major Thompson with a letter to Gen. Gage asking that they be pardoned and restored to their duties.

Nothing else appears upon which any suspicion of his political principles could be based. But public opinion sometimes seems to need very little tangible foundation, and it was unalterably set against him. Envy, hatred, malice, and all uncharitableness pursued him from all sides. There was nothing wrong in particular, but he was in that position which is most nearly hopeless in practical politics; he was "in wrong." In the summer of 1774 he was summoned before a committee of the citizens of Concord on the charge of being unfriendly to American liberty. No proof was found, he denied the accusation, and was discharged. But

3

the hostility of his neighbors continued to increase, and in November, by the advice and assistance of his brother-in-law, Judge Timothy Walker, he left his wife and child and secretly went back to Woburn, whence he wrote to his father-in-law Dec. 24:

"Reverend Sir. The time and circumstances of my leaving the town of Concord have, no doubt, given you great uneasiness, for which I am extremely sorry. Nothing short of the most threatening danger could have induced me to leave my friends and family; but when I learned from persons of undoubted veracity, and those whose friendship I could not suspect, that my situation was reduced to this dreadful extremity, I thought it absolutely necessary to abscond for a while, and seek a friendly asylum in some distant part.

"Fear of miscarriage prevents my giving a more particular account of this affair; but this you may rely and depend upon, that I never did, nor (let my treatment be what it will) ever will do any action that may have the most distant tendency to injure the true interest of this my native country. * * *

"The plan against me was deeply laid, and the people of Concord were not the only ones that were engaged in it. But others, to the distance of twenty miles, were extremely officious on this occasion. My persecution was determined on, and my flight unavoidable. And had I not taken the opportunity to leave the town the moment I did, another morning had effectually cut off my retreat."

January 11, 1775, he wrote in reply to Parson Walker's letter urging him to return to Concord, * * * "As to any concessions that I could make, I fear that it would be of no consequence, for I cannot possibly, with a clear conscience, confess myself guilty of doing anything to the disadvantage of this country, but quite the reverse."
* * *

But peace was not in Woburn. He was arrested there May 15, 1775, on the same indefinite charges. Again no proof was produced, and he was discharged. This second prosecution was undoubtedly instigated by reports from Concord, or from New Hampshire soldiers at Cambridge. Smarting under prosecution which his conscience told him was groundless, and discouraged by its persistence, he turned to the camp of Washington's army at Cambridge in the hope that his military rank might be recognized, and that he might be given a command in the American army which would reinstate him in public favor. Unsuccessful in this he endeavored to establish himself in the business of supplying non-commissioned officers' epaulets for the army, and again he found hostile influences too powerful for him to overcome. In his letter of August 14 he wrote "I have been driven from the camp by the clamours of the New Hampshire people." There was no other way to turn for justice. Civil life and the military camp alike were permeated with hostility towards him, and on the 13th of October, 1775, he left Woburn in company with his step-brother, and took refuge on board the British frigate Scarborough in the harbor of Newport, a Royalist by compulsion of the Revolutionists.

As to the real allegiance of his heart and mind, I present these extracts from his letter of Aug. 14, 1775, to Rev. Timothy Walker, his wife's father:

* * * "I am not so thoroughly convinced that my leaving the town of Concord was wrong (considering the circumstances at the time) as I am that it was wrong in me to do it without your knowledge or advice. This, Sir, is a step which I have always repented, and for which I am now sincerely and heartily sorry, and ask your forgiveness.
* * *

"I was peculiarly happy in having my brother Walker's approbation of my conduct. But notwithstanding he thought me innocent, yet he dared not appear in my behalf; he saw the current was against me, and was afraid to interfere. * * *

"As to my being instrumental in the return of some deserters by procuring them a pardon, I freely acknowledge that I was. But will you give me leave to say that what I did was done from principles the most unexceptionable, the most disinterested, a sincere desire to serve my King and country, and from motives of pity to those unfortunate wretches who had deserted the service to which they had voluntarily and solemnly tied themselves, and to which they were desirous of returning. * * *

"But as to * * * maintaining a long and expensive correspondence with G(overno)r W(entwor)th or a suspicious correspondence, to say the least, with G(overno)rs W(entwor)th and G(ag)e, I would beg leave to observe that, at the time Governor Wentworth first honored me with his notice, it was at a time when he was as high in the esteem of his people in general as was any Governor in America, at a time when even Mr. Sullivan was proud to be thought his friend. * * *

" 'Tis true, Sir, I always thought myself honored with his friendship, and was even fond of a correspondence with him, a correspondence which was purely private and friendly, and not political, and for which I cannot find it in my heart to either express my sorrow or ask forgiveness of the public.

"As to my maintaining a correspondence with Governor Gage, this part of the charge is entirely without foundation, as I never received a letter from him in my life; nor did I ever write him one, except about half a dozen lines which I sent him just before I left Concord may be called a letter, and which contained no intelligence, nor anything of a public nature, but was only to desire that the soldiers who returned from Concord might be ordered not to inform any person by whose intercession their pardon was granted them. * * *

"And notwithstanding I have the tenderest regard for my wife and family and really believe I have an equal return of love and affection from them; though I feel the keenest distress at the thoughts of what Mrs. Thompson and my parents and friends will suffer on my account; and though I foresee and realize the distress, poverty, and wretchedness that must unavoidably attend my pilgrimage in unknown lands, destitute of fortune, friends, and acquaintances, yet all these evils appear to me more tolerable than the treatment which I meet with from the hands of mine ungrateful countrymen."

"I must also beg a continuance of your prayers for me, that my present afflictions may have a suitable impression on my mind, and that in due time I may be extricated out of all my troubles. That this may be the case, that the happy time may soon come when I may return to my family in peace and safety, and when every individual in America may sit down under his own vine, and under his own fig-tree, and have none to make him afraid, is the constant and devout wish of

Your dutiful and affectionate son

Benj^a Thompson."

His talents were lost to America at a time when they were most needed. His genius for organization was driven to a foreign soil when it should have been devoted to the establishment of a new government in the land of his birth; and all this because a few of his friends and relatives in Concord did not have the courage to stand with him, face his jealous accusers, and declare his innocence in accordance with their belief. As a people and as individuals we can never cease to regret that so unworthy motives as jealousy and suspicion deprived America in her time of need of the services of the greatest social scientist of his day, founder of a new school of social economy that taught the world how to care for the poor by teaching the poor how to care for themselves, the vital principles of which endure to this day.

His genius was officially recognized by the United States government in an invitation in 1799 to return to America and organize the Military Academy at West Point, and he was at the same time offered the commission of inspector-general of artillery in the United States army. This invitation he was obliged to decline on account of his official obligations to the Bavarian government, and his labors in the founding of the Royal Institution of Great Britain. In appreciation of the invitation he left, by his will, all his books, plans, and designs relating to military affairs to the United States Military Academy.

In 1774, when Gen. Gage found quarters lacking for his troops in Boston, and sought to provide for his men by building new barracks, he was much embarrassed by the fact that the carpenters of Boston and vicinity had joined the American forces and withdrawn from the city. Consequently he was obliged to send into the country for the necessary skilled workmen. Gov. John Wentworth, in a letter to the Earl of Dartmouth dated Nov. 15, 1774, says: "General Gage having desired me to furnish some carpenters to build and prepare quarters for his Majesty's troops in Boston, the carpenters there being withdrawn, and the service much distressed; I immediately engaged and sent him a party of able men, which arrived to the General, and are very useful."

This was in October, 1774, and the news of the sending of the artificers to Boston soon spread abroad. Nicholas Austin of Middleton was suspected of being an agent of the Governor in engaging and forwarding the carpenters. The muster of militia which was held in Rochester the first week in November afforded an opportunity for these rumors and suspicions to crystallize, and the Sons of Liberty proposed to visit Mr. Austin in a body and ascertain the truth. But some of the cooler and more conservative among them, fearing hasty and violent action if this plan should be carried out by the people in their excitement, proposed that Mr. Austin be requested to meet the Sons of Liberty at some time and place to be agreed upon. Wise counsel prevailed, and the latter plan was adopted. The Rochester committee of correspondence notified Mr. Austin to meet them at the house of Stephen Wentworth, innholder, in Rochester on the following Tuesday, Nov. 8.

On the day appointed a large concourse of the people of Rochester and the neighboring towns met to hear the case. Mr. Austin appeared, and after taking oath before John Plummer, Esq., gave a rather lame statement of his part in the affair. He testified that he spoke to only four

of the men hired for Gen. Gage, and told them to go to Gov.
Wentworth and speak to him; that he did not tell the men
they were to go to Boston, although he suspected that to be
the case from a remark the Governor had made; that the
Governor told him the people would be dissatisfied when the
affair became known, but, thinking it would be best, he had
proceeded; that he told the men the general of the army
would pay them their wages.

Mr. Austin was then forced to his knees in full view of the
assembly, and compelled to sign and repeat the following
confession and declaration:

"Before this Company I confess I have been aiding and
assisting in sending men to Boston to build Barracks for the
Soldiers to live in, at which you have Reason justly to be
offended, which I am sorry for, and humbly ask your Forgiveness, and I do affirm that for the future I never will be
aiding or assisting in any Wise whatever in Act or Deed
contrary to the Constitution of the Country, as Witness,
my hand."

And he was not, for no record of any further action
against him is found. He represented Wakefield, Middleton, and Effingham in the convention to consider the
Federal constitution in 1788, and was a member of the
House of Representatives the same year.

Eleazer Russell, long time postmaster of New Hampshire
and naval officer of the port of Portsmouth, read the Association Test literally as an obligation to do active service,
for which he was physically incapacitated. He also had a
strong element of Quakerism in his character, and a sense of
honor which would not allow him to do a popular deed in violation of his moral principles. He explained his refusal to
sign the Association Test in a letter to Meshech Weare, chairman of the Committee of Safety, Aug. 17, 1776, in which he
said:

"On the 4th day of May last, Coll Wentworth, of the
Committee for the Town of Portsmouth, brot me the Association to Subscribe, At a time I was so ill as to be in-

capable of any thing. Upon growing better, I thot largely of the matter, and, finding my mind perplex'd, wrote him on the Subject; which letter, at my request, he consented to lay before the Honora^ble Committee of Safety.

"Till yesterday I never knew but the Association paper, with my letter, had been in the Committees hands for more than two months: And now I find myself bound by every principle of Honor, Duty, and gratitude to enlarge upon the Affair.

"It was, and is, meerly to secure the morality of my mind that I was reluctant to put my name to it—Solemnly to bind my-self to the performance of what nature & necessity rendered impossible, I started at the thot of. And, tho my health is mended, So wreckd Are my nerves that I could not do one hours Military Duty to Save my life.

"The Article of shedding human blood, in me, is not a humor, but a principle—not an evasion, but a fact. It was received in early life, and has 'Grown with my growth & Strengthend with my Strength'—not a partiality for British more than Savage blood, For, al circumstances considered, I think the latter more innocent than the former.

"From the first Injuries done America by Great-Britain, my thots took fire on the Subject; And have been conceived & uttered, in one unvaried Strain, To the highest personage and down to the meanest enemy, without hesitation or reserve, So that I can challenge all mankind to impeach me to my country.

"To enlarge on the matter in my own favor would be easy, but might appear indelicate, and to be Wholly Silent in the case would be criminal.

"Therefore believing my conduct is to be judg'd by persons of Liberal Sentiments and Sentiments of mind—I am, with the greatest respect, Honorable Sir

"Your obliged & dutiful Hum^e Servt

E Russell."

James Sheafe, one of the fifteen men arrested in Portsmouth, had no further trouble with the Revolutionists during the war, and became United States Senator from New Hampshire in 1801. But in his political campaigns he was severely reminded by Gen. Sullivan of his doubtful principles during the Revolution.

Joshua Atherton of Amherst, an able lawyer, and a wealthy, educated, and cultured gentleman, was opposed to the war because he believed that the result could not be other than disastrous to the colonies, and that, in the end, they would not only fail to gain relief from any of the oppression under which they labored, but would add a burden of debt, and be subjected to whatever vindictive measures might be enacted upon a conquered people. He suffered some persecution, but his tact and unfailing good-nature saved him from much more. He was in custody for nearly a year and a half, and in prison so much of that time that his health was permanently injured. After the war he resumed his practice, and filled the office of representative to the General Court, delegate to the convention to consider the Federal constitution, State Senator, and Attorney-General. But his reputation as a Royalist was always a bar to his gaining the full confidence of the people, and for the last 13 years of his life he was a physical and mental invalid.

Among those who declined to sign the Association Test because they considered themselves bound in honor by oath of office under the Crown was Theodore Atkinson. A member of an old, wealthy, and aristocratic family of Portsmouth, he was connected with the Royal government in New Hampshire in some capacity, civil, military, or judicial, nearly all his life after graduating from Harvard College in 1718. At the outbreak of the war he was Secretary of the province, a position he had held continuously since 1741, except from 1762 to 1769, when the office was filled by his son, Theodore, Jr., and he was also Chief Justice of the province, having been appointed in 1754. He had married Hannah, daughter of Lieut.-Gov. John Wentworth, and was accordingly a brother-in-law of Gov. Benning Wentworth, and, by marriage, an uncle of Gov. John Wentworth, the last Royal Governor. Sabine calls him a Royalist, but a careful examination of the case shows that his sense of honor did not allow him to violate his official oath, and that after his office was taken away from him he maintained a strict neutrality which was respected by his townsmen.

In July, 1775, the Provincial Congress sent a committee to remove the records of the province from Portsmouth inland to Exeter for greater safety, as the defences of Portsmouth were not capable of repelling the British ships of war which were daily expected. When the committee called upon Secretary Atkinson July 4 for the records of his office, he refused to deliver them, saying that such an act would be contrary to his honor and his oath of office. In a letter to Gov. Wentworth describing the incident the Secretary says: "After an hour's moderate conversation, and without any heat, the Committee left me, and I was in hopes I should not have any farther visit from them, but on the sixth instant they came again and urged the delivery. I still refused as before, and told them they well knew it was not in my power to defend the office by force of arms; if they took the records etc., or any of them, they must be answerable. They then entered the office, and took all the files and records belonging to the Secretary's office, except those books in which were recorded the several charter grants of land, which were with your Excellency to take some minutes from. The Committee offered me their receipt, agreeable to their orders from the Congress, but I refused, being no otherwise concerned than barely as a spectator. They then cleared the office of all the books and papers, and transported them to Exeter, where they are (I am informed) to remain until further orders."

On the second visit of the committee the Secretary made a written reply to their demands, which he filed in the archives, where it remains to this day.

"In answer to your request touching my delivery of the records and files belonging and now in the Secretary's office of the Province, I beg leave to acquaint you that I am by his Majesty's Special Commission appointed Secretary of this Province during his Majesty's pleasure & my residence in the Province, and agreeable thereto I was Admitted and sworn into that office and had the keeping of the archives belonging thereto deliver^d to me and put under my Direction & in my keeping. You cannot but see my Honour and my Oath forbids my consent or even my connivance in such a Delivery, unless accompanied with his Majesty's supercedent or my not being in this Province. Gentlemen—the Difficulties, I may say the Distresses in the Province, & indeed of the whole Continent are such that every cause of additional Perplexity need be avoided. I have, Gentlemen, no tho^{ts} of attempting to maintain the security of the Records in my custody by force—this I know would have no good effect; my aim is only to remove any grounds of complaint that may be against me for either Neglect or mal-Practice in the Execution of my said office." Major William Weeks was chairman of the committee, and in a letter to Gov. Wentworth dated July 10, 1775, the Secretary says, "Major Weeks seemed sorrowful that he was appointed."

Judge Atkinson was at this time 77 years old, and respected, honored, and beloved throughout the province. He retired to private life, and no suggestion of slander or suspicion was ever brought against his name. He was not spared to see the outcome of the struggle, but died in Portsmouth Sept. 29, 1779.

To introduce a very different and far less attractive kind of Royalist, let me cite the case of Major Batcheller. Breed Batcheller of Nelson, son of John, was born in Wenham, Mass., Dec. 11, 1740. At the age of 16 he served in Capt. John Burke's Falltown company in the Crown Point expedition of 1756. He was also in service the following year, and in the campaigns of 1758 and the Crown Point expedition of 1759 in Capt. William Paige's Hardwick company. His father died in Brookfield, Massachusetts, June 10, 1765, leaving him some property, and the same year he went to Nelson, then an unsettled town, where he purchased nearly 9000 acres of land as a speculation, and afterwards added to it large tracts in Marlborough and Hollis. Within ten years he had established a tavern and built the only grist mill in town.

Breed Batcheller was an arrogant, blustering, profane, purse-proud man, a man of many enemies, and always in trouble. He refused to sign the Association Test, probably because all his neighbors did sign it, and because he feared the result of rebellion or a revolution on his property. When the news of the battle of Lexington reached Nelson the local militia hurriedly assembled and marched to Cambridge. Major Batcheller was the ranking officer in the town, but instead of taking command he hastened off to Keene, ostensibly to find out if the rumor of the battle were true. He followed his men tŏ Cambridge and spent several weeks there, but merely as a spectator, as the officers and men refused to recognize his authority. His allegiance was already under suspicion. About the time of the Boston Tea Party he had defied public opinion by bringing home from Canada a quantity of India tea and offering it for sale in Nelson and surrounding towns.

In December, 1775, he was summoned before the town committee of safety, and, though he appeared, he refused to answer any of their questions and denied their jurisdiction.

Josephine Rugg testified that Major Batcheller damned the committee and threatened to kill the first man that should come to take him.

Jonathan Felt heard him say the committee should not come into his house, but might stand at the door and talk to his hogs, and that he would be tried by fire and brimstone before he would be judged by the committee.

Meanwhile Major Batcheller continued his tea-selling trips, and complaints were made by various town committees of safety to the General Court. The failure of the Nelson committee to lodge him in jail caused the town, at a meeting held Sept. 17, 1776, to appoint a new committee, and the major was soon brought to jail in Keene. His case came before the House of Representatives March 20, 1777, and he was placed under bonds of £500 and confined to the town limits of Nelson on parole. His bounds were afterwards enlarged to allow him to visit his lands in Marlborough.

This was altogether too much freedom to suit his fellow-townsmen; they protested most strenuously, and renewed their efforts for his imprisonment. Their petition for a new trial was granted. New evidence was introduced, upon which he was ordered to be closely confined until further order of the General Court or Committee of Safety. Witnesses testified that he swore that if a mob came after him he would stick the small pox into them, though he would not give it to a dog; that he would rather be hanged than come under an independent government; that he damned Col. Hale and the Congress, and said he would rather be tried by hell-hounds than by the committee; that he drank the King's health and damnation and confusion to the States.

But notwithstanding his profanity and violent language, some of which is too vile for repetition, he was neither a Royalist nor a Revolutionist at heart, but was solely concerned about the effect of war on his property, as many witnesses testified that he said he would be very glad if the differences between the King and the colonies could be settled without bloodshed on either side.

Although sentenced, he was not yet in prison. He was hunted like a wild beast, and lived for some time in a cave not far from his home still known as "Batcheller's den," where he was supplied with food by his wife and a kind-hearted neighbor. Tradition says that one day his pursuers, being weary, sat down to rest directly over his cave, and so near that he could hear their terrible threats. Convinced that only by escape from the country could he save his life, he fled, so closely followed that he was obliged to clamber down the face of an almost perpendicular cliff by a narrow, winding cleft since called "Batcheller's stairs." He joined Burgoyne's army, and was made a captain in the Queen's Rangers. His company formed a part of Col. Baum's force at Bennington, where he was severely wounded in the shoulder. He was sent to Canada with the other wounded, and afterwards returned to New York, where he remained until the close of the war. Then he went with the British troops to Digby, Nova Scotia, and followed a life of dissipation. In 1785 he fell out of his boat in the Annapolis basin, and was drowned. His wife and five children were left in Nelson in destitute circumstances, but were allowed a home and a small allowance by the State out of his confiscated estate.

Dr. Eleazer Wheelock, founder of Dartmouth College, was accused of Toryism for no other reason than that in 1775 he celebrated Thanksgiving at the college on the 16th of November instead of the 30th. The 16th was the date established in the Connecticut proclamation, which he received first; and as the New Hampshire proclamation had often failed to reach him until after the day named therein, he had been accustomed to observing some day in November most convenient to himself and the college. "But," he says, "I soon heard there was a great clamor in the neighborhood * * * and that it was spreading fast abroad as though we were like to be all undone; that I should be speedily sent for to Exeter, 150 miles, to answer for it before the Congress as a Tory." The clamor was so great that he finally consented to preach another sermon on the 30th. This only made matters worse, and the Doctor says "a doleful smoke we have." To clear up the smoke he was obliged to call upon the committees of safety of Hanover, Lebanon, Plainfield, and Cornish, who completely exonerated Dr. Wheelock, and charged John Paine of Hanover with the responsibility for the slander.

There were other Royalists quite as distinguished, as interesting, as picturesque, as any I have mentioned, though perhaps not as available as types of certain classes. Among these were Col. John Fenton, member of the General Court from Plymouth, who took refuge in the house of Gov. Wentworth, and was persuaded to come forth only by planting a cannon in the street before the house, and bringing it to bear on the front door; and Major

Robert Rogers, explorer, adventurer, soldier, and the best Indian fighter in New England, who has come down to us in story and legend as a hero of those strenuous days; but he was, in truth, a man sadly devoid of moral principle, of whom his wife Elizabeth, daughter of Rev. Arthur Browne of Portsmouth, said in her petition for divorce in 1778, that at the time of their marriage in June, 1761, he was "a person of some Character and distinction (tho' your petitioner married him solely in Obedience to the will of her parents, friends, etc.)." Then follows her sad story of desertion six days after the marriage, his infidelity, debauchery, and drunkenness, which the General Court found to be true, and granted the divorce.

But we had other Royalists than our own in New Hampshire, and more of them. During the last three months of 1776 231 Royalists, mostly from Albany and Dutchess counties, were exiled from New York to New Hampshire. Others were sent to Massachusetts, Connecticut, and Pennsylvania. There were not prisons enough in New York to hold all those under arrest, and the committees for detecting conspiracies thought that by sending them away from their homes and scattering them abroad many conspiracies might be prevented, and the possibilities of organization much lessened. Before sending any to New Hampshire the committee asked the advice of Lieut.-Col. Joseph Welch, who was in command of two companies of Col. Thomas Tash's regiment of New Hampshire militia, doing guard duty at Fishkill during the session of the New York convention. Col. Welch replied that he had no doubt the State of New Hampshire would willingly aid the State of New York in this matter to the extent of her ability.

According to the statements made by these men, many of which are on file in our archives, they were arrested, in many cases without warrants, confined without specific charges against them; and sent without notice 250 miles on foot to Exeter without sufficient clothing, money, or any of the necessaries required on such a journey through the wilderness. They came in small parties under guard, and on arrival at Exeter were delivered to the State Committee of Safety for disposal. The commanding officer of each guard bore a list of the prisoners in his charge, and on these lists those considered by the New York committee as the most dangerous were marked for close confinement, and were committed to jail in Exeter, Dover, and Amherst. The others were allowed to take lodgings in any but the seaport towns on any terms they could make, and at their own expense.

The New Hampshire government was far more lenient in its treatment of the New York Royalists than of its own. Many were allowed under bonds to return home, or to go to friends and relatives in Massachusetts and Connecticut. When those in jail escaped they were not strenuously pursued. By the end of 1777 they were all gone.

On the 18th of November, 1776, a party of more than a hundred New York Royalists passed through Worcester, Massachusetts, on the way to New Hampshire. The pitiful sight of these wretched, shivering, foot-sore exiles produced such an effect on the people of Worcester that the Committee of Safety, sitting that day, passed a most remarkable resolution.

This very long document says in part: " * * * as the resolve of the state on the 8th day of May, 1775, was a temporary provision, and has had its operation; as the resolution of our predecessors in office, disarming and confining to this town a number of its inhabitants, was expressly to prevent their joining our avowed enemies, and to deprive them of the means of obstructing measures adopted for the common defense: * * * as this day's spectacle of wretched, deluded objects, the ruined, exiled grovelings, spued out from a sister State, is a serious warning to persons sporting with the feelings of an whole continent, be they whom, where, or what they may; and the Worcester jail, filled with the same engaging geniuses will remain a standing memento of future dangers to the unfriendly; as the Congress for the continent have supposed that there were some from weakness deceived, others from apprehen-

sions that British power was irresistable, frightened into
opposition, and have recommended such as subjects for
kindness, reason, and reformation; * * * as, early in
the dispute, when the expediency of measures was the topick
of the day, possibly a mere difference in opinion was the
too slender grounds of some hasty suspicions, and a sub-
sequent change of sentiment and conduct may have laid
the foundations for forgiveness and friendship, which are
equally Christian and political duties; * * * as the
restraining of an Englishman to a single town is in derogation
of common right, depriving him of his arms an infraction on
liberty, and recording him a Tory stamping him with in-
famy, and cannot be justified but upon principles of publick
necessity: * * * Therefore

"Resolved, That it is inexpedient that the resolution
of the late Committee of this town, disarming and confining
a number of its inhabitants, be any longer in force, that
such persons once more be put upon a standing with the
rest of their fellow-Countrymen; that they be allowed the
privileges of Englishmen, of friends to their country, of
passing where and when they please, until they evidence by
their conduct and behaviour a different character; and
that such as have arms in the possession of the Committee
may receive the same by making application to Mr. Bald-
win, their chairman.

"2dly, Resolved, That it be recommended to all true,
firm and tried friends to their country to endeavor to convince persons of every degree, character, and complexion,
that the cause we are engaged in is of too much dignity to be
sullied by rashness, too important, too seriously important,
to be weakened by tumult, divisions, and party strife;
that liberty received strength and vigour from prudence
and consideration; that justice, equity, regularity, and, in
some instances, moderation, are her closest friends; that
she courts virtue as her bosom companion, and shuns vice
as her dangerous enemy; and therefore, equally avoiding
feverish fits of political heat and cold, banishing from their
breast all personal prejudices, private piques, narrow opin-

4

ions, illiberal distinctions, and unbecoming jealousies; displaying a magnanimity proportional to the importance and danger of the struggle, cultivating harmony of sentiment and unanimity of councils, and carefully distinguishing between the friend and the foe, that it is wisdom (acting discreetly, firmly, unitedly, and spiritedly) to receive all such to their favour, friendship, and confidence who will give ample and satisfactory assurances of their readiness to join in the defence of their much-injured country, and their steady, persevering attachment to her glorious cause; at the same time to exercise a vigilant attention to those who secretly influence under the principles of an affected neutrality, and those who may labour to conceal themselves under the despicable cloak of a cunning duplicity, if any such there be.

"3rdly, Resolved, That it be recommended to the good people of this town that they use their utmost endeavors immediately to equip themselves with every implement of war, as the necessary means of defence from a foreign attack or an internal insurrection."

A sad sight must have been seen, and a sad state of affairs must have been realized, to have brought forth from a Committee of Safety, legally constituted guardian of the liberties of its constituents, such a powerful description of the havoc wrought to the American cause by unjust and hasty suspicion, personal enmity, and unfortunate misunderstanding, all masquerading in the garb of patriotism, and such a masterly exposition of the attitude of the Revolutionists as it should have been. A great sense of right and justice, and a strong belief in their final victory run through the whole, seeking to expand ideas which were narrow, and to overthrow methods begotten of a first instinctive fear and consequent hasty action.

It is not my purpose to attempt a partisan defense of the Royalist, but only to present some facts which seem to disprove the popular idea that he was a raging fiend with a cloven hoof and a forked tail. The Royalists were Americans, like the Revolutionists; socially, intellectually, morally, they were like their opponents, no worse, no better. They had no national, state, or other civil organizations. The whole Royalist party in the colonies was made up of individuals here and there, of all classes, of all stations in life, who did not wish, for various reasons, to dissolve their allegiance to the Crown. A general definition of the Royalist of the Revolutionary period would be one who did not agree with the majority on the main issue of the time; and the fact of that difference of opinion constituted him a traitor in the eyes of that majority. We forget, as our forefathers did, that it was the Revolutionist, not the Royalist, who was seeking to overthrow an established government, and that the Royalist was the man who refused to violate his oath of allegiance to the government under which he had been born and had grown to man's estate. That the Revolutionists were justified 'we can have no doubt, but that did not deprive the Royalist of the right to hold to his own opinion so long as he did not interfere with the rights of others. When he did seek to interfere with the purposes of the Revolutionists by becoming active in the cause of the enemy, then, and not until then, did he become guilty of treason under American law. All the Revolutionists were traitors under English law, but they freed themselves from the operation of that law by their victory in arms.

Viewing the Tory as one who opposed the government under which he lived in time of war, have we not had them in every war? I doubt if there has been a war in the history of civilization in which there have not been, in the territory of each side, some sympathizers with the enemy. To go no farther back than the memory of this generation, the Mexican war was opposed by the entire Whig party; there were Tories in the War of the Rebellion; they were called Abolitionists in the South and Copper-Heads in the North. In the Spanish and Philippine wars there were Tories, but they were called Anti-Imperialists. It is a great commentary on the change which growth, prosperity, and success have wrought in the spirit of this nation that the Royalists of the Revolution were arrested, tried, and imprisoned, while the Anti-Imperialists were allowed to publicly give moral aid and encouragement to an enemy in arms against the government of the United States without the slightest molestation, either official or private, while that government went on its chosen way with calm and dignified toleration.

It is to the credit of the people of New Hampshire that persecution of the Royalists never reached the extreme, never caused the loss of life nor permanent physical injury to any human being. There were no serious riots. Whatever abuses they suffered were due to that undercurrent of lawlessness which exists in every community at all times, and always breaks forth in some degree in time of war, pestilence, fire, famine, flood, or any other great and overwhelming calamity.

Henry Guy Carleton, in one of his plays, "Ye Earlie Trouble," a delightful play which was born in Boston and died there, caused one of his characters, an irascible old Tory, to say: "When rebels are successful they become patriots." There is much of truth in this cynical remark. All revolutions must begin in rebellion, in an uprising and a conflict against the existing order of things, an order which has so far failed to shape itself to the ways of human progress as to create and foster a sense of discontent and discord in the hearts of the people, which develops into appeal, protest, and finally war, when all other means of reparation have failed, and all other sources of justice have been exhausted. Then, if the rebellion is successful, the old order of things is swept away, giving place to new, and he who was active and helpful in the change is hailed as a patriot by the new government he has helped to establish, and he is held in honor and esteem by his people. If a rebel is successful he becomes a patriot, but an unsuccessful rebel remains a rebel forever.